STAYING IN TUNE

WITH

GOD

STAYING IN TUNE

WITH

GOD

MY PRAYER

Father God, I pray that You will touch the hearts and minds of everyone who reads this book. I pray that the messages shared in this book will minister to their spirits and enhance their lives. Most importantly, I pray that each person will develop a closer relationship with You. Amen.

PASTOR LARRY NICKERSON

Glimpse of Glory Christian Book Publishing
P.O. Box 94131
Birmingham, Al 35220

Unless otherwise noted Scriptures are taken from King James Version Bible.

ISBN: 978-0-9833221-5-3

Printed in the United States of America

CONTENTS

SPECIAL THANKS

To my Heavenly Father:
First and foremost, I want to thank You Lord for calling, anointing and appointing me to be Your servant, to preach the Gospel to the lost souls. You have given me the wisdom, knowledge and understanding to pour into the lives of Your people. I know that I cannot do anything without you. I will continue to give You all the glory.

To my wife:
Yolanda Marshall-Nickerson, I thank God for answering my prayer concerning sending me a true helpmate. You have taken your rightful place to help birth what God has placed within me. Words can never express my gratitude for you. I will love and cherish you forever.

To my children and my grandsons:
Kiarra, Larry Jr., Latoya, Marvin, Marcus, Joshua, Isaiah, Jeremiah and Gabriel III, thank you all so much for being supportive. All of you will always hold a special place in my heart. I love each of you.

To my family:
I want to thank my mother, Sylvia Jenkins, who recently went home to be with the Lord. She was such a blessing in my life.

She was and will (even from Heaven) always be my cheerleader. She started pushing me when I was a little boy. She made sure I went to church and learned about my Heavenly Father. To my siblings, Sherman, Robert, William, and Glenda, thank you all for your love, prayers and support. A special thanks to my brother, Pastor Samuel Nickerson, who has also gone home to be with the Lord. I thank you for passing the torch so that I may run this race in ministry. You left your mantle with me on the day you departed this earth. I will be forever grateful for the relationship we had. I cannot forget my three aunts, Aurelia, Mattie, and Viola, thank you all so much for being an inspiration in my life. To my cousin, Cynthia, thank you so much for always been in my corner and supporting me from the beginning of my journey.

To all of my friends:
I am thankful for the true friends who have always supported and encouraged me to excel in life. Edward, Ivan, Billy, Clarence and Minister Allen Love, you all are very special friends who have had my best interest at heart.

To In God We Trust Ministries Overseers:
Apostle Johnny Hughes and wife, Pastor Sherry Hughes, I want to thank you all for being a blessing to my church family. My wife and I look up to you both. You all are great leaders in the Body of Christ. The both of you epitomize excellence in ministry. Your thoughts, prayers, love and support mean so much to me.

To Eastlake Church of God in Birmingham, Alabama:
Mr. Billy Rush and wife, Pastor Patricia Parker-Rush, I want to thank you all for opening your doors to allow God to use me to exercise my spiritual gifts. Thank you both for your words of encouragement. Your act of kindness and generosity will always be remembered.

INTRODUCTION

As a child of God, it is important to stay connected and in tune with Him. It is a privilege and honor to be connected to the One who created us in His image. Because we were made in His image, we are to take on His character and let our light shine so brightly in the earth, helping those who are lost to get to know the same merciful, forgiving, kind, giving, caring and loving God who, from the beginning of time, "Loved us so much that He gave His only begotten Son, that whosoever believeth in him should not perish, but have everlasting life."

God has given us His Word to help us develop a closer walk with Him, grow spiritually, have a balanced life and be equipped to handle adversity—and stay in tune with Him as He leads the way and make "every crooked place straight" in our lives. We should not only read His Word, but we should live by it. Each of us must learn to pray, meditate, fast and submit our will to His.

As we…submit to His will, He will provide every need we have, answer every prayer request, move every stumbling block that the enemy puts in our path, position us "in the right place at the right time," and allow us to experience all of His wonderful, matchless benefits.

1

HEARING THE VOICE OF GOD

As you stay in tune with God, you will learn how to hear His voice.

God wants to talk to us every day. It is an honor and privilege to hear God's voice. We need to always have our ears opened to hear His voice. We need to also be ready to receive in our hearts what He speaks to us at any given time. There are many ways you can hear God's voice. I would like to share with you three of those ways.

The first way to hear His voice is through prayer. Prayer is one of the most effective ways to hear God's voice. It is a two-way communication. When you communicate to God through your sincere prayers, He will in turn communicate back to you, answering those petitions and prayers that you bring before Him. You have to pray to God without ceasing, and you can never pray too much. When you pray to God, you are also spending time with Him. This is the foundation of building a true relationship with Him. As you spend time with God, He will teach you how to discern Satan's traps. He will show you what direction you need to take in life, and He will tell you things that are instrumental to your spiritual growth.

The second way to hear His voice is by reading and studying His Word. It is important that you read and study God's Word in order to advance in life. The Word of God is your guide. Every situation you will ever encounter in life, there is a solution provided in His Word. You have to make time to read and study the Word of God daily. There may come a time when you will read God's Word, and you may not understand it or get a revelation, but you must continue reading it until it marinates in your spirit. After reading and studying His Word over and over again, you will gain a clearer understanding.

The third way to hear His voice is through His servants, Pastors. The Bible says in Jeremiah 3:15, "And I will give you Pastors according to mine heart, which shall feed you with knowledge and understanding." God has already assigned you a spiritual leader; therefore, you need to allow Him to lead you to that leader who will help nourish and develop the gifts within you so that you can be effective in the Kingdom of God.

MEDITATE ON GOD'S WORD

Scriptures to read:

John 10:27
My sheep hear my voice, and I know them, and they follow me.

Jeremiah 29:11
For I know the thoughts that I think toward you, says the Lord, thoughts of peace and not of evil, to give you a future and a hope.

Jeremiah 29: 12-13
Then you will call upon me and go pray to me, and I will listen to you, and you will seek me and find me, when you search for me with all your heart.

Proverbs 3:5-6
Trust in the Lord with all your heart and lean not to your own understanding; in all your ways acknowledge Him and He shall direct your path.

Habakkuk 2:1
I will stand upon my watch, and set me upon the tower, and will watch to see what He will say unto me…

~NOTES~

2

GOD IS IN CONTROL

As you stay in tune with God, you will realize that your ways are not His ways.

God desires that each of us be a living sacrifice. He wants to live through us; therefore, we must yield ourselves to Him. You may have a hard time yielding to Him because you feel that you know what is best for your life. When you think that you are in control of your life, you will do things your way and not even consider God. You must learn to relinquish your thoughts and your ways to God. He knows all about you, and He desires to lead you on our journey in life. You cannot go anywhere nor do anything without God.

God is your eyes, your ears, your voice, and your thoughts—He is in total control of your life. You have to stay connected to God if we want to continue growing and experience His benefits. If you are not connected to Him, you will be out of control. You will not have any sense of direction. You will be lost, thinking your way is the right way.

If you allow God to stay in control of your life, your path will be clearer because He will be the One ordering your steps. And when God is leading the way, you will have no room for error. You will experience happiness, peace, an overflow of joy, His unconditional love, and a better understanding of the things of God.

MEDITATE ON GOD'S WORD

Scriptures to read:

Psalm 37:4
Delight thyself in the Lord; and he shall give thee the desires of thine heart.

Proverbs 19:21
There are many devices in a man's heart; nevertheless the counsel of the Lord, that shall stand.

Proverbs 16:9
A man's heart deviseth his way: but the Lord directs his steps.

Psalm 115:3
But our God is the heavens: he hath done whatsoever he hath pleased.

Ephesians 1:11
In whom also we have obtained an inheritance, being predestinated according to the purpose of him who worketh all things after the counsel of his own will.

~NOTES~

3

GOD IS POSITIONING

As you stay in tune with God, you will appreciate whenever He positions you.

When God positions you, you will not only be on time, you will be right where you need to be in His timing. You will never have to question God's doing when He positions you because He knows exactly where He desires for you to be at a certain point in your life. He will confirm every move that you make, giving you peace within your spirit as you follow His lead.

You will be able to leave your comfort zone and allow God to lead you without any hesitation, knowing that He will position you in the right place for your breakthrough, deliverance, increase, healing, promotion, etc. You will have full confidence and assurance that it is Him and no one else who is leading you; therefore, He will be the only One who will get the Glory.

I want you to know that God may allow you to experience discomfort and pain while He is preparing to position you in the right place…you may encounter something disturbing in your home, on your job, in your church, etc. Think it not strange if you face obstacles while God is trying to position you. He will give you the strength that may propel you in a position where He desires...He will open doors that you will be able to freely walk through, and "no man will be able to close them."

MEDITATE ON GOD'S WORD

Scriptures to read:

John 1:5
And the light shineth in darkness; and the darkness comprehended it not.

Psalm 143:8
Cause me to hear thy lovingkindness in the morning; for in thee do I trust: cause me to know the way wherein I should walk; for I lift up my soul unto thee.

Psalm 16:9
Therefore my heart is glad, and my glory rejoiceth: my flesh also shall rest in hope.

Psalm 17:5
Hold up my goings in thy paths, that my footsteps slip not.

Psalm 37:23
The steps of a good man are ordered by the LORD: and he delighteth in his way.

~NOTES~

4

OPPOSITION

As you stay in tune with God, you will be able to face and conquer opposition.

The closer you get to God and make up your mind that you are going to live for Him for the rest of your life, opposition will occur. You will encounter things for the very first time—things the devil will use to steal your focus, joy and peace, and take you off course. You cannot give any place to the devil. You cannot allow him to discombobulate you. You have to take control of your mind and cast down any thoughts of being consumed by whatever the opposition may be. You cannot entertain his tactics nor listen to his crafty, deceitful, wicked voice.

You have to listen to God and follow His guidance in order to deal with certain situations in your life. When you are in tune with Him, you won't even have to worry about opposition getting the best of you. God will help you to conqueror anything that is designed to destroy you mentally, socially, physically or spiritually. He will help you to stay focused and show you how to keep your joy and peace in the midst of any opposition.

He will even connect you with positive people who will help strengthen and encourage you to do what is right when you are faced with opposition—people who will encourage you not to give up; those who will push you; those who will pray with you; those who will labor with you; those who will speak life into you.

I want you to always remember that Jesus conquered the world, and He has given you the power to conqueror opposition. You already have the victory.

MEDITATE ON GOD'S WORD

Scriptures to read:

Romans 8:28
And we know that all things work together for good to them that love God; to them who are the called according to his purpose."

Romans 8:31
If God be for us, who can be against us?

Roman 8:35
Who shall separate us from the love of Christ…shall tribulation, or distress cr persecution, or famine, or nakedness or peril or sword."

Hebrews 12:3
For consider him that endured such contradiction of sinners against himself, lest ye be wearied and faint in your minds.

~NOTES~

5

ACCOUNTABILITY

As you stay in tune with God, He will help you understand the importance of accountability.

God will make sure you are accountable in everything you do and say. You are to live your life in a way that will be pleasing unto Him. You have to understand that God is watching every move you make and hearing every word you speak—when people don't see and hear you, God does. You have to "Let your light so shine before men, that they may see your good works, and glorify your Father which is in heaven" (Matthew 5:16).

When you have poor, negative behavior and your actions are not consistent with His Word, then you are not pleasing God. You are not bringing Him honor nor are you glorifying Him. You are not making Him proud to say that you are His faithful servant; you are bringing Him shame, and God is not going to let any of His children shame Him.

You have to understand that you were made in His image and you represent Him, so you must do all things well. Sure, you may fall short of His glory sometimes, but He wants you to get back up and produce good fruit. What I mean by this is that you are to represent Him in a loving, kind, responsible way, touching and making a difference in the lives of people; effectively witnessing to others who may not know the way—and, you must strive to lead a godly life, being the best example of Him.

If you are struggling in the area of accountability, God will help you, give you grace to stand firm on His Word, and make sure you grow so you that you can be a more effective Christian. God will connect you with people who have your best interest at heart—those who you can be accountable to and they can be accountable to you, too. When you are accountable to another brother or sister in Christ, they will not only tell you when you are right; they will tell you when you are wrong, too. They will also build you up and not tear you down and throw you in a 'lion's den' for a fault or shortcoming you may be dealing with. They will encourage you to get back on course, repent and "run the race that is set before you."

I want you to know that God is also accountable to us. God keeps His Word. He will honor His Word when people fail and turn their back on you. He will never default on His promises. He will never leave you. He will make sure that you have more than enough. He will pick you up when you fall. He can be counted on during your toughest and roughest times in life. You can trust Him.

MEDITATE ON GOD'S WORD

Scriptures to read:

Galatians 6:1
Brethren, if a man be overtaken in a fault, ye which are spiritual, restore such an one in the spirit of meekness; considering thyself, lest thou also be tempted.

James 5:16
Confess your faults one to another, and pray one for another, that ye may be healed. The effectual fervent prayer of a righteous man availeth much.

Hebrews 10:25
Not forsaking the assembling of ourselves together, as the manner of some is; but exhorting one another: and so much the more, as ye see the day approaching.

Philippians 2:4
Look not every man on his own things, but every man also on the things of others.

~NOTES~

6

CONFUSION OF THE MIND

*As you stay in tune with God, you will learn how to cast down
those negative thoughts that lead to confusion.*

You are a child of God and He wants you to have a clear,
free, peaceful mind as you journey through life. "He is not the
author of confusion, but of peace" (1 Corinthians 14:3). God
wants to renew your mind and get you to focus on the things of
Him so that you can experience His peace every day—reading
His Word daily will help you to feel His presence and His
peace.

You will also begin to feel good about yourself, and if
you feel good about yourself, you are going to think positive,
do positive things, surround yourself with positive people and
do as His Word says, "whatsoever things are true, whatsoever
things are honest, whatsoever things are just, whatsoever things
are pure, whatsoever things are lovely, whatsoever things are of
good report; if there be any virtue, and if there be any praise,
think on these things" (Philippians 4:8). By doing these things,
you will develop a sound mind, too.

Now the devil does not want you to have peace. He also
does not want you to think on those things which will uplift

your spirit; therefore, he is going to try to bring confusion to your mind as often as he can so that he can overtake you. One of the most effective ways he confuses the mind is through negative minded people. You cannot entertain negative people because those will be the ones who will try to bring negative conversation to you, and through those conversations you will find yourself being drained mentally, emotionally and spiritually. It is a way for the devil to shut you down and steal your peace and focus. You have to reject and cast down everything that is not like God.

MEDITATE ON GOD'S WORD

Scriptures to read:

John 14:26
 But the Comforter, which is the Holy Ghost, whom the Father will send in my name, he shall teach you all things, and bring all things to your remembrance, whatsoever I have said unto you.

Philippians 2:5
Let this mind be in you, which was also in Christ Jesus.

2 Timothy 1:7
For God hath not given us the spirit of fear; but of power, and of love, and of a sound mind.

2 Corinthians 10:5
Casting down imaginations, and every high thing that exalteth itself against the knowledge of God, and bringing into captivity every thought to the obedience of Christ…

~NOTES~

7

UNDERSTANDING YOUR PURPOSE

As you stay in tune with God, you will understand that you have a purpose in life.

You will realize that it is something different and unique about you the more you spend time with God. As you begin to talk to God, you will become close to Him, and He will begin to call you by your name. When God calls you by your name, then you know that you are special to Him and that He is trying to get your attention to do something.

God will give you instructions for you to follow, and you have to obey His instructions as they will lead you to your greater if executed. His instructions are a direct link to your purpose which He will reveal to you. You were created to fulfill a purpose in life. God will start giving you small tasks to see how you handle them, and then it will progress into something big over a period of time. This is when you will find yourself going from one level to the next.

God will give you a vision and take you step by step until it is fully manifested. He will show you the end; that is why His Word says that "your latter shall be your greater." You won't find out how great your purpose is until you start carrying it out.

God will be well pleased with you when you start walking in your purpose because you will no longer sit back waiting on others to do what He has put inside of you to do. A great feeling comes after understanding what your purpose is. I want you to understand that people will be impacted by your purpose. You will make a positive difference in the lives of others as you carry out your purpose.

MEDITATE ON GOD'S WORD

Scriptures to read:

John 15:8
Herein is my Father glorified, that ye bear much fruit; so shall ye be my disciples.

John 15:16
You did not choose me, but I chose you and appointed you that you should go and bear fruit and that your fruit should abide, so that whatever you ask the Father in my name, he may give it to you.

Acts 26:16
But rise and stand upon your feet, for I have appeared to you for this purpose, to appoint you as a servant and witness to the things in which you have seen me and to those in which I will appear to you.

~NOTES~

8

YOU HAVE BEEN CHOSEN FOR GREATNESS

As you stay in tune with God, you will be able to discover the greatness in you.

The Bible says, "Before you were thought about being conceived, God knew you…" When your mother gave birth to you, God had already purposed you to be great in the earth. So, despite the voice the devil used to tell you that you would never be anything in life, God still has a plan for your life, and He calls you great.

There is greatness connected to you and through you. It is the Great One who lives deep within your spirit and will be there until the end, and because He lives on the inside of you, you have all you need to succeed in every area of your life. He has given you power in your tongue to speak life into your dry situation and command great things to happen for you.

When you speak life and tap into the greatness that is on the inside of you, then you will no longer limit yourself and/or be moved by the negative voices that say you cannot do it. It is all about what God says about you and what He already equipped you with before you were conceived. There are many gifts that He planted on the inside of you when you were a fetus, and those gifts are for you to use while you are in the earth, for His glory. "Your gifts will make room for you..." They will help propel you toward your greater—greater is the destiny that God has for you, His child.

You have to understand that as a child of the Most High God, you can do anything with Him on your side. So, even as you walk through the valleys of life and encounter trial and tribulations, and experience setbacks and disappointments, there will still be greatness inside of you. Those gifts are there, and you are getting ready to give birth to them—one by one. You will move forward in this season of your life and experience your greater.

MEDITATE ON GOD'S WORD

Scriptures to read:

Luke 1:15
 For he shall be great in the sight of the Lord…

1 John 4:4
Greater is He that is in you than he that is in the world...

Matthew 19:26
But with God all things are possible.

Philippians 4:13
I can do all things through Christ which strengtheneth me.

~NOTES~

9

BE MADE WHOLE

As you stay in tune with God, you will be able to receive mental, emotional, physical and spiritual healing.

The Bible says that there was a certain man who had an infirmity thirty-eight years, and when Jesus saw him lying there by the pool, He knew that the man had been in that condition for a long time. Jesus asked the man, "Do you want to be made well?" Some of you may be like the man at the pool of Bethesda. You have been dealing with a certain situation and/or had an infirmity for a long time, and you are ready to be made whole.

Wholeness is available to all of God's children. You must stay focused on the promises of God that are outline in His Word. Isaiah 53:5 declares that we are healed by His stripes; therefore, we are not only limited to physical healing, but God can and will heal any of us in whatever capacity we need it—we can receive emotional, mental, and spiritual healing, too.

I want you to know that God is ready to make you complete. No matter what issues you have in your life, He will make you whole. He will give you peace that surpasses all understanding. He will give you the joy you have desired for a long time. He will give you strength to endure the difficult times that you will encounter in life.

You have to stay connected to God to receive all of His benefits, and healing is just one of the many benefits that He has for His children.

MEDITATE ON GOD'S WORD

Scriptures to read:

Luke 8:50
But when Jesus heard it, he answered him, saying, Fear not: believe only, and she shall be made whole.

Colossians 2:10
And ye are complete in him, which is the head of all principality and power...

Thessalonians 5:23
And the very God of peace sanctify you wholly; and I pray God your whole spirit and soul and body be preserved blameless unto the coming of our Lord Jesus Christ.

~NOTES~

10

PATIENCE

As you stay in tune with God, you will learn how to be patient.

It is not uncommon for you to want things to manifest in your life as quickly as possible after you have waited for such a long time. You are probably tired of waiting, right? You may even be at the brink of throwing in the towel. You may have had the thought, "I wonder why it has not happened for me yet."

I have good news! Just because it has not come to fruition, does not mean that God has not heard your prayers or forgotten about you. You have to understand that God has a particular time for things to happen in your life. It is not like He cannot do it for you; it is that He is trying to teach you how to wait for Him to move and bring it to pass in His timing.

While you are waiting, go ahead delight yourself in Him, submit to His will, and continue trusting and believing that He will give you desires of your heart. And, "Commit thy way unto the Lord..." (Psalm 37:5). After you commit your way unto Him, allow Him to develop your character, strengthen your heart, renew your mind, remove some things (bitterness, unforgiveness, anger, strife, jealousy, etc.) that are not like Him, and do a new thing in and through you. Sometimes you have to go through a cleansing process and be perfected before what you are seeking God for manifests in your life. You will be more than excited and mentally, emotionally, and spiritually ready when God brings it to pass.

MEDITATE ON GOD'S WORD

Scriptures to read:

Psalm 27:14
Wait for the Lord; be strong, and let your heart take courage; wait for the Lord!

Psalm 37:7
Rest in the LORD, and wait patiently for him: fret not thyself because of him who prospereth in his way, because of the man who bringeth wicked devices to pass.

Galatians 5:22-23
But the fruit of the Spirit is love, joy, peace, patience, kindness, goodness, faithfulness, gentleness, self-control; against such things there is no law.

Galatians 6:9
And let us not be weary in well doing: for in due season we shall reap, if we faint not.

Habakkuk 2:3
For the vision is yet for an appointed time, but at the end it shall speak, and not lie: though it tarry, wait for it; because it will surely come, it will not tarry.

Isaiah 40:31
But they that wait upon the Lord shall renew their strength; they shall mount up with wings as eagles; they shall run, and not be weary, and they shall walk and not faint.

Revelation 14:12
Here is the patience of the saints: here are they that keep the commandments of God, and the faith of Jesus.

~NOTES~

11

A FIGHT TO REACH DESTINY

As you stay in tune with God, He will make sure you reach your destiny in spite of the obstacles you may encounter.

Does it seem like every time you try to get ahead there is something pulling you back? Are stumbling blocks in your path? Does it appear that you have more enemies than friends? Do you feel like "the world is against" you sometimes? Do you feel like you are always in a spiritual fight, warring against demons that you cannot even see? Do you feel like your battles have been back to back? If you answered "Yes" to any of these questions, I want to let you know that you should "Not be afraid or discouraged…the battle is not yours, but God's. (2 Chronicles 20:15).

You are destined to succeed and do great things in the earth. When you are seemingly doing everything right to get to where God intends for you to be in your life, you will find yourself in a fight. The devil will launch attacks to impede your progress. You will suffer persecution. You will be lied on. You will be mistreated. You will be talked about. You will be overlooked and rejected by people. You will be hurt. You will endure pain. But, even after facing all these things, you do not have to fret. "Fear not nor be dismayed, be strong and of good courage." You can count it all joy because everything is going to still work together for your good, according to Romans 8:28.

You will reach destiny because it is God's will for your life. All you have to do is keep the faith, trust Him wholeheartedly, pray without ceasing, read His Word, obey His instructions and submit to His will, and let Him fight all of your battles.

MEDITATE ON GOD'S WORD

Scriptures to read:

Ephesians 1:11
In him we have obtained an inheritance, having been predestined according to the purpose of him who works all things according to the counsel of his will.

Ephesians 6:11
Put on the whole armour of God, that ye may be able to stand against the wiles of the devil.

James 4:7
Submit yourselves therefore to God. Resist the devil, and he will flee from you.

Luke 10:19
Behold, I give unto you power to tread on serpents and scorpions, and over all the power of the enemy: and nothing shall by any means hurt you.

1 John 5:4
For whatsoever is born of God overcometh the world: and this is the victory that overcometh the world, [even] our faith.

Romans 8:37

... In all these things we are more than conquerors through him that loved us.

Psalm 91:11

For he shall give his angels charge over thee, to keep thee in all thy ways.

~NOTES~

12

THE JUST SHALL LIVE BY FAITH

As you stay in tune with God, you will be able to activate your faith and apply it to every situation.

Sometimes in life God will allow you to go through certain situations to help you activate your faith. The Word of God says, "Without faith it is impossible to please Him." The only way you can gain faith and apply it to any situation you may encounter is that you need to have a personal relationship with God and read His Word because "Faith comes by hearing the Word of God."

There is a story that I would like to direct you to in the Bible. It is what I would refer to as the faith story of Shadrach, Meshach, and Abednego. These three men were thrown in a burning fiery furnace because they would not serve, bow down and worship an image that King Nebuchadnezzar set up. The three men had faith that God would deliver them and He did. (Read Daniel-Chapter 3).

Another story that I would like to direct you in the Bible is the one about the woman with an issue of blood. She did not live a normal life during the time she dealt with this issue; she was plagued by this infirmity for 12, long years. The Bible says she went from one physician to the next. Her situation remained the same until she had an encounter with Jesus. All she had was her faith when she laid eyes on Jesus the day she got healed of her disease. She touched the hem of Jesus' garment and instantly she was healed. He told her that her faith made her whole. (Read Luke-Chapter 8:43-48).

As you can see, faith is very instrumental to having your situation turned around. You may be in a spiritual fight right now. You may be facing a storm that has yet to cease. You may be having family issues that you need God to fix. You may be sick in your body. You may be at a standstill and nothing has changed about your circumstances. The reason you may not see the results you have been praying about is because you have been operating in fear. God wants to see your faith in order to move in the way you desire and need for Him to. He is ready to move on every situation that you are dealing with. It is time to read and stand firm on His Word and activate your faith.

MEDITATE ON GOD'S WORD

Scriptures to read:

Hebrews 11:1
Now faith is the substance of things hoped for, the evidence of things not seen.

Hebrews 11:6
But without faith it is impossible to please him: for he that cometh to God must believe that he is, and that he is a rewarder of them that diligently seek him.

James 1:6
But let him ask in faith, nothing wavering. For he that wavereth is like a wave of the sea driven with the wind and tossed.

Romans 10:10
For with the heart man believeth unto righteousness; and with the mouth confession is made unto salvation.

Mark 10:52
And Jesus said unto him, Go thy way; thy faith hath made thee whole. And immediately he received his sight, and followed Jesus in the way.

2 Corinthians 5:7
For we walk by faith, not by sight.

~NOTES~

13

THE PROMISE

As you stay in tune with God, you will experience all of His promises.

One source defines promise as "a declaration or assurance that one will do a particular thing or that a particular thing will happen." As you journey in life, people will make promises to you. They will promise to buy you gifts. They will promise to support you. They will promise to be there for you in time of need. They will promise to give you money. They will promise so many things, and they will not keep their promise. They will let you down, some intentionally and some unintentionally. God does not want you to put your trust in people. He wants you to put your trust in Him. People will leave and forsake you, lie and deceive you, but "God will never leave or forsake you." You can count on Him to stand behind His Word.

It is God's desire that all of His children experience His promises that are "Ye and Amen." He promises to supply all of our needs according to His riches and glory; that means He has everything to take care of us. We have to believe that He will deliver on every promise that He has made.

I want you to understand though that there is a process to your promise. God may have shown you in a dream and/or allowed someone to prophesy that you are going to get a job promotion, an increase, start a business, get married, etc. Just because it has not happened for you yet, does not mean it is not going to happen. Sometimes you may have to encounter things before your promise actually manifests in your life. It's almost as if a certain trial is required before you receive your promise.

God has to also prepare your mindset to receive the promise He has just for you. He wants to clear your mind of all negative thoughts and ideas. He wants to speak to your mind and cause it to think on those things that are pure, holy and positive. In essence, your mind needs to be renewed in order to receive the promises of God.

MEDITATE ON GOD'S WORD

Scriptures to read:

Psalm 84:11
For the LORD God is a sun and shield: the LORD will give grace and glory: no good thing will he withhold from them that walk uprightly.

1 John 2:25
And this is the promise that he hath promised us, even eternal life.

2 Peter 1:4
Whereby are given unto us exceeding great and precious promises: that by these ye might be partakers of the divine nature, having escaped the corruption that is in the world through lust.

Matthew 11:28
Come unto me, all ye that labour and are heavy laden, and I will give you rest.

Philippians 4:19
But my God shall supply all your need according to his riches in glory by Christ Jesus.

~NOTES~

14

AGAPE LOVE

As you stay in tune with God, you will learn of His love, be filled with His love and execute His love.

God loves us so much that, even from the beginning of time, "...He gave His only begotten Son, that whosoever believeth in him should not perish, but have everlasting life." This is a special kind of love that only He can give. It is pure, honest, real and unconditional. God's love for you does not change; it is always the same. "God's love never fails and it will never cease."

You can experience His love at all times. When you fall short of His glory, He still loves you. When you make a mistake, He still loves you. When you aren't as committed to going to church, reading your Bible, praying, giving, fasting and being faithful to the things of God, He still loves you. Even when you think that you are not worthy, He still loves you.

God wants to fill you with His love and teach you how to love unconditionally. When you form a relationship with Him, obey His commandments, and follow His instructions, He will make sure His love flow through your heart like "rivers of living water."

He encourages us to love each other, too. The Word of God says, "Be completely humble and gentle; be patient, bearing with one another in love." He cares about how you exemplify His love toward others because you are representing Him. You have to understand that others will know that you are His child through the love that you show towards them, even those who use and mistreat you. His love in you should be executed in every aspect of your life.

MEDITATE ON GOD'S WORD

Scriptures to read:

John 3:16
For God so loved the world, that he gave his only begotten Son, that whosoever believeth in him should not perish, but have everlasting life.

1 John 4:7
Beloved, let us love one another: for love is of God; and every one that loveth is born of God, and knoweth God.

Mark 12:31
And the second is like, namely this, Thou shalt love thy neighbour as thyself. There is none other commandment greater than these.

Romans 13:10
Love worketh no ill to his neighbour: therefore love is the fulfilling of the law.

Romans 12:9
Let love be without dissimulation. Abhor that which is evil; cleave to that which is good.

Colossians 3:14
And above all these things put on charity (love), which is the bond of perfectness.

~NOTES~

15

THE JOY OF THE LORD

As you stay in tune with God, you will be filled with His everlasting joy.

You may be dealing with something in your life that has stripped your joy. Perhaps, it could be a job loss, a promotion that you were overlooked for, separation or divorce, betrayal of a friend, hurt from church members, family issues, death, and the list goes on.

As you journey through life, you will experience these kinds of things, and they will cause you to feel hopeless, depressed, oppressed, sad, lonely, etc. You must realize that even during the times that you face situations that may not be working in your favor; your joy will remain strong because "The joy of the Lord is your strength." And it takes a measure of strength to go through some of life's situations.

I want you to know that as you encounter these things, you can go to that secret place and talk to God. What I mean by this is that you can go to a quiet place in the comfort of your home and lay all of your cares and concerns before God. He will talk to you, listen to you, and fill the emptiness in your life with His joy. Yes, God will fill your heart, mind and soul with everlasting joy.

You must understand that life is more meaningful when you have the joy of the Lord on your side. You will be able to face life's situations in a different light, and embrace the changes of life head on with a smile and a sense of hope.

MEDITATE ON GOD'S WORD

Scriptures to read:

Psalm 16:11
Thou wilt shew me the path of life: in thy presence is fullness of joy; at thy right hand there are pleasures for evermore.

Psalm 4:7
Thou hast put gladness in my heart, more than in the time that their corn and their wine increased.

Psalm 126:3
The LORD hath done great things for us; whereof we are glad.

1 Chronicles 16:27
Glory and honour are in his presence; strength and gladness are in his place.

Nehemiah 8:10
…For the joy of the LORD is your strength.

Isaiah 55:12
For ye shall go out with joy, and be led forth with peace.

~NOTES~

16

GOD'S GRACE

As you stay in tune with God, you will experience His grace.

Have you ever experienced a trial in your life that you thought would never end? Do you remember the time you fell short of God's glory? Do you remember how He kept you while you were in the midst of your mess? Have you ever been sick to the point where you thought you were going to die, but God healed your body? If you answered "Yes" to any of these questions, I want to let you know that it was God's grace that stepped in and turn things around for you.

He turned things around for me when I was at the brink of death back in 2012. I had two back to back major surgeries. I was hospitalized for nearly two months. The doctor told me that I had pulse in my body for over 30 years and he didn't see how I was even still alive. But, God!

I needed the grace of God, and it was His grace that not only healed my body, but it was His grace that saved my life. I found out that it was "sufficient enough" just as His Word tells us. Oh, His grace is something that we don't deserve, but Jesus shed His blood for us all; therefore, we were able to receive grace. God is not selfish by any means. He not only shows us grace every day; He has mercy on us, too. I am so glad about it, and you should be, too.

MEDITATE ON GOD'S WORD

Scriptures to read:

2 Corinthians 12:9
And he said unto me, my grace is sufficient for thee: for my strength is made perfect in weakness. Most gladly therefore will I rather glory in my infirmities, that the power of Christ may rest upon me.

Ephesians 2:8
For by grace are ye saved through faith; and that not of yourselves: it is the gift of God.

James 4:6
But he giveth more grace. Wherefore he saith, God resisteth the proud, but giveth grace unto the humble.

Romans 3:24
Being justified freely by his grace through the redemption that is in Christ Jesus.

2 Corinthians 13: 14
The grace of our Lord Jesus Christ be with you all. Amen.

2 Corinthians 9:8

And God is able to make all grace abound toward you; that ye, always having all sufficiency in all things, may abound to every good work.

Titus 3:7

That being justified by his grace, we should be made heirs according to the hope of eternal life.

~NOTES~

17

GOD INHABITS YOUR PRAISE

As you stay in tune with God, you will find out how much He inhabits your praise.

You have to learn how to give God praise even when you cannot trace Him or feel His presence. When you are at the brink of giving up, you must still give God praise. When your money is low and you don't know where your next meal will come from, you still must give Him praise. When your friends turn their back on you, there is still a need to praise God. When your family members disown you, give God praise anyhow. When you are going through problems on your job, praises are still due Him. The Bible says, "Let every thing that hath breath praise the LORD. Praise ye the LORD" (Psalm 150:6).

We owe Him praise for who He is, for what He has done in our lives, and for what He is going to do—what our eyes have yet to see. I want you to know that God inhabits your praise. When you praise Him, you are showing Him how much you adore, honor, love, and appreciate Him. I believe that God stands on His throne and smile when He sees the sincere praise of His people.

I want to encourage you to never allow anything or anyone to stop you from giving God praise. The more you praise Him, the more He will begin to release blessings to you. He will begin to open doors for you. He will begin to move stumbling blocks out of your path. He will begin to turn some things around for you. He will begin to do some things in your life that you'd have never imagine could be done. Keep praising God, through the good and the bad times.

MEDITATE ON GOD'S WORD

Scriptures to read:

Psalm 30:4
Sing unto the LORD, O ye saints of his, and give thanks at the remembrance of his holiness.

Psalm 86:12
I will praise thee, O Lord my God, with all my heart: and I will glorify thy name for evermore.

Psalm 145:2
Every day will I bless thee; and I will praise thy name for ever and ever.

Psalm 113:3
From the rising of the sun unto the going down of the same the LORD's name is to be praised.

~NOTES~

18

YOU ARE LOST WITHOUT GOD

As you stay in tune with God, you will find that He will guide you through life.

If you are traveling to a particular city, town or state for the first time without a map or GPS, then you may find yourself asking someone for direction. The person you ask may not be for certain. They may give you directions that could lead you to the wrong place; therefore, you will be lost. You will then find yourself having to ask someone else for directions to help you get to your destination.

Have you ever tried to find a particular location and got lost? If so, I am certain you felt uneasy and nervous, especially if you were alone. You probably told yourself you would never do that again without knowing where to go and how to get there. You probably even thought that if you had a map or GPS you would not have gotten lost. I agree.

I want to let you know that just as you can be physically lost when trying to find a place without having a map or GPS, you can be spiritually lost if you do not know God and have a personal relationship with Him. When you are spiritually lost, you will easily yield to sin. You will live a life of disobedience, doing things that are contrary to His Word. You will have no sense of direction in life. You may find yourself being tossed up and down, going in circles, wandering in the wilderness, and dealing with the same issues over and over again.

You do not want to live a life without God—He is the "way, truth and life." If you do not already know Him, I want to encourage you to get to know Him and allow Him to order your steps. You will never have to worry about God giving you the wrong directions; you can rest assure that He will always steer you in the right direction.

MEDITATE ON GOD'S WORD

Scriptures to read:

John 3:17
For God sent not his Son into the world to condemn the world; but that the world through him might be saved.

John 6:44
No man can come to me, except the Father which hath sent me draw him: and I will raise him up at the last day.

1 Corinthians 6:19-20
Or do you not know that your body is a temple of the Holy Spirit within you, whom you have from God? You are not your own, for you were bought with a price. So glorify God in your body…

Ephesians 2:12
That at that time ye were without Christ, being aliens from the commonwealth of Israel, and strangers from the covenants of promise, having no hope, and without God in the world.

Psalm 10:17
LORD, thou hast heard the desire of the humble: thou wilt prepare their heart, thou wilt cause thine ear to hear

~NOTES~

19

STAND AND ENDURE UNTIL THE END

As you stay in tune with God, He will give you the strength to stand and endure until the end.

Sometimes when facing certain situations in life, to stand...can be the hardest thing for someone to do. With the cloudy days, long nights, storms raging, and high winds blowing in your life, you are probably thinking where your strength will come from to stand this time around.

I want you to think about how God brought you through that last trial; how He fought that last battle for you; how He "showed up and showed out" that last time; how He provided your need when you could not see your way; how He gave you strength when you were feeling weak; how He allowed you to hold on when you were at the brink of giving up.

God gave you the power to stand then, and He will help you to stand in the midst of what you are going through right now. He will give you power to conquer whatever the enemy throws in your direction. He will make a way for you when you least expect it. No matter how difficult things may become, God will give you the strength to stand and endure until the end.

MEDITATE ON GOD'S WORD

Scriptures to read:

1 Corinthians 16:13
Watch ye, stand fast in the faith, quit you like men, be strong.

2 Timothy 2:3
Thou therefore endure hardness, as a good soldier of Jesus Christ.

Matthew 24:13
But he that shall endure unto the end, the same shall be saved.

1 Corinthians 15:58
Therefore, my beloved brethren, be ye stedfast, unmoveable, always abounding in the work of the Lord, forasmuch as ye know that your labour is not in vain in the Lord.

Philippians 4:1
Therefore, my brethren dearly beloved and longed for, my joy and crown, so stand fast in the Lord, my dearly beloved.

Ephesians 6:11
Put on the whole armour of God, that ye may be able to stand against the wiles of the devil.

~NOTES~

20

THE WORD

As you stay in tune with God, you will able to identify the distractions that may prevent you from reading your Word or going to church to hear the preached Word of God.

There is a solution to every single thing that you will ever deal with in life. Your solution is in a very rich, fulfilling, powerful...book, the Bible. You have to read it, believe it and obey what it says, in order to grow spiritually. You can also gain knowledge, understanding, wisdom, strength...from the Word of God.

God has even thought enough of you to give you pastors according to His heart that will feed you knowledge and understanding. (Read Jeremiah 3:15). God will speak to your pastor and give him or her the Word you need for your situation; that is why it is so very important to attend your place of worship (church). The Bible says, "Not forsaking the assembling of ourselves together..." (Hebrews 10:25)

You can rest assure that if you continue to abide in His Word, and attend church as often as you can, you will receive whatever it is that you need and/or desire. Perhaps, you may be praying, seeking and believing God for a breakthrough, a promotion, a financial turnaround, a spouse, or a number of other things. I want you to know that it is going to happen for you, and I must encourage your faith to believe God for these things.

You can depend on God to honor His Word because He is His Word. He will never default on His Word. Isaiah 55:11 says, "So shall my word be that goeth forth out of my mouth: it shall not return unto me void, but it shall accomplish that which I please, and it shall prosper in the thing whereto I sent it."

MEDITATE ON GOD'S WORD

Scriptures to read:

John 1:1
In the beginning was the Word, and the Word was with God, and the Word was God.

2 Timothy 2:15
Study to shew thyself approved unto God, a workman that needeth not to be ashamed, rightly dividing the word of truth.

Hebrews 4:12
For the word of God is quick, and powerful, and sharper than any two-edged sword, piercing even to the dividing asunder of soul and spirit, and of the joints and marrow, and is a discerner of the thoughts and intents of the heart.

Psalm 119:105
Thy word is a lamp unto my feet, and a light unto my path.

Isaiah 40:8
The grass withereth, the flower fadeth: but the word of our God shall stand for ever.

James 1:22

But be ye doers of the word, and not hearers only, deceiving your own selves.

2 Timothy 3:16

All scripture is given by inspiration of God, and is profitable for doctrine, for reproof, for correction, for instruction in righteousness.

Psalm 33:4

For the word of the LORD is right; and all his works are done in truth.

~NOTES~

A CALL TO SALVATION

After God created the world, He decided to create man to have dominion over the earth. He realized that man needed a helpmate, and from man a woman was formed. Just as God desires for the man and woman to have an intimate relationship with each other, He also wants us to have an intimate relationship with Him.

Man and woman fell into sin and there became brokenness in our relationship with God. God is forgiving. God is merciful. He sent His only beloved son, Jesus, in this world to die for the sins of the world and through His bought blood which was shed on Calvary's Cross; Salvation became available for you and me. All we have to do is what Romans 10:19 says, and that is 1) Confess with our mouth Jesus is Lord and 2) Believe in thine heart that God raised Him (Jesus) from the dead, then thou shall be saved. In doing this, we form that relationship with the Creator just like it was in the beginning. It's a personal relationship with the Father.

To develop a closer walk with God, there are steps we must take too. We must pray and fast often; spend time reading the Word, getting to know His will through His Word. When we know His Word, we will know the Father's heart and the will for our lives; submit to God's will and not ours. I encourage you to take up your cross and follow Him from this day forward.

ABOUT THE AUTHOR

Pastor Larry Nickerson is a native of Birmingham, Alabama. He is married to Yolanda Marshall-Nickerson. He is the leader of In God We Trust Ministries in Birmingham, Alabama. He is the third of seven siblings and the father of seven and the proud grandfather of two. He loves to spend time with his family.

Pastor Larry loves the Lord with all his heart. He was called into the ministry at the age of 33. He realizes that he is destined for greatness. He is an anointed man of God and has a passion to bring healing and deliverance and rebuild and restore lives by ministering the Word of God.

Pastor Larry holds a Bachelors Degree in Rehabilitation Counseling with a minor in Theology from Faith Grant College. He also has an Associate Degree in Computer Science from Southern Junior College of Business.

www.ingramcontent.com/pod-product-compliance
Lightning Source LLC
Chambersburg PA
CBHW060359050426
42449CB00009B/1808